IØ136476

Anonymous

Annual report of the Society of American Taxidermists

Anonymous

Annual report of the Society of American Taxidermists

ISBN/EAN: 9783337716851

Printed in Europe, USA, Canada, Australia, Japan

Cover: Foto ©ninafisch / pixelio.de

More available books at **www.hansebooks.com**

SOCIETY

OF

ᴀMERICAN ᴛAXIDERMISTS

Mᴀʀᴄʜ 24ᴛʜ, 1880, ᴛᴏ Mᴀʀᴄʜ 25ᴛʜ, 1881.

RᴏᴄʜᴇꜱTᴇʀ, N. Y. :

DAILY DEMOCRAT AND CHRONICLE BOOK AND JOB PRINT, 3 WEST MAIN ST.

1881.

SOCIETY

OF

AMERICAN TAXIDERMISTS.

Organized March 24th, 1880.

OFFICERS.

PRESIDENT.

FREDERIC S. WEBSTER, - - - - - of Rochester, N. Y.

VICE-PRESIDENT.

THOMAS W. FRAINE, - - - - - - of Rochester, N. Y.

SECRETARY.

WILLIAM T. HORNADAY, - - - - - of Rochester, N. Y.

TREASURER.

FREDERIC A. LUCAS, - - - - - - of Rochester, N. Y.

EXECUTIVE COMMITTEE.

JOHN MARTENS, - - - - - - - of Rochester, N. Y.
A. B. BAKER, - - - - - - of Syracuse, N. Y.
T. T. SOUTHWICK, - - of Rochester, N. Y.

Members of the Society.

HEDLEY, Mrs. GEORGE H. - - - - - - Medina, N. Y.

HEDLEY, CHARLES H. - - - - - - - Medina, N. Y.

HORNADAY, WILLIAM T. - - - - - - Rochester, N. Y.

HUTCHISON, GEORGE F. - - - - - - - Rochester, N. Y.

JENCKS, FRED. T. - - - - - - - - Providence, R. I.

LUCAS, FREDERIC A. - - - - - - - Rochester, N. Y.

MARTENS, JOHN - - - - - - - - Rochester, N. Y.

MÜHL, GEORGE - - - - - - - - Rochester, N. Y.

MYHILL, A. - - - - - - - - - Medina, N. Y.

NICHOLAS, GEORGE LAWRENCE - - - - - - Princeton, N. J.

ORMSBEE, E. L. - - - - - - - - Cleveland, Ohio.

OSBORNE, W. C. - - - - - - - - New York, N. Y.

PARK, AUSTIN F. - - - - - - - Troy, N. Y.

RATHBUN, S. F. - - - - - - - - Auburn, N. Y.

ROGERS, T. B. - - - - - - - Wilmington, Del.

ROWLAND, THOMAS - - - - - - - - Paterson, N. J.

SCOTT, Prof. W. E. D. - - - - - - - Princeton, N. J.

SMITH, WILLIAM G. - - - - - - - - Rochester, N. Y.

SMITH, Miss E. - - - - - - - - Rochester, N. Y.

SOUTHWICK, T. T. - - - - - - - Rochester, N. Y.

SPENCER, F. W. - - - - - - - - Spencerport, N. Y.

SUMNER, Dr. CHARLES R. - - - - - - Rochester, N. Y.

TOWNSEND, C. H. - - - - - - - - Beatty, Penn.

WARD, HENRY L. - - - - - - - - Rochester, N. Y.

WATSON, JAMES S. - - - - - - - Rochester, N. Y.

WALLACE, JOHN - - - - - - - New York, N. Y.

WEBSTER, FREDERIC S. - - - - - - Rochester, N. Y.

WOOD, A. H. - - - - - - - Painted Post, N. Y.

WOOD, NELSON R. - - - - - - - Rochester, N. Y.

WRIGHT, FRANK S. - - - - - - Auburn, N. Y.

(45 Active Members .

FIRST

COMPETITIVE AND GENERAL EXHIBITION

OF THE

Society of American Taxidermists.

Rochester, N. Y., Dec. 14-18, 1880.

All the honors to be awarded before disclosing any exhibitor's name to the Judges.

JUDGES.

Prof. J. A. ALLEN, of the Museum of Comparative Zoölogy, Cambridge, Mass.
Dr. JOSEPH B. HOLDER, of the American Museum of Nat'l History, New York City.
Mr. W. E. D. SCOTT, of the Princeton College Museum, Princeton, N. J.

List of Honors to be Awarded:

To best piece in entire exhibition, - - - -	Silver Medal.
To second best piece in entire exhibition, - . -	Bronze Medal.*
To best general exhibit, - - - - -	Bronze Medal.
To second best general exhibit, - - - -	Diploma of Honor.
To *each exhibit* in *Class A,—Taxidermy proper*,—which shall stand at 85 or over, a - - -	Diploma of Honor.
To *each exhibit* in *Class A*, which shall stand at 75 and under 85, a - - - - - -	Certificate of Merit.
To Grotesque Groups and animals grotesquely mounted, Diplomas and Certificates will be awarded at the discretion of the Judges.	
To the handsomest article of ornament or use, -	Diploma.
To the second handsomest article of ornament or use, -	Diploma.
To the best exhibit of Accessories to Taxidermy, in each section,	Diploma.
To second best in the same, at the discretion of the Society, -	Certificate.

* This Medal is not provided for in the Constitution, but by a majority of members it is considered necessary, and the question of its being awarded will come before the Society in the general meeting.

LIST OF POINTS AND VALUES

For the Judgment of Specimens at the Exhibitions of the Society of American Taxidermists.

Groups of Mammals.

General difficulty of subject, . . .	15
Attitude, ...	15
General artistic effect,	. 15
Size of specimens, .	10
Neatness of finish,	. 10
Form, ...	10
Expression, . . .	. 10
Smoothness, ...	5
Naturalness of colored parts,	5
Quality of natural surroundings,	5
Perfection, . .	. 100

Single Mammal Specimens.

General difficulty of subject, .	. . 15
Attitude, ...	15
Form and proportions, .	. 15
Size of specimens, . . .	15
Development of muscles,	. 10
Expression, ...	10
General neatness of finish,	. . 10
Smoothness, ...	5
Naturalness of colored parts,	. 5
Perfection, .	. 100

Groups of Birds

General difficulty, . . .	. 15
Attitude, ...	15
General artistic effect, .	. 15
Size of specimens, ...	15
Natural surroundings and effects,	. 15
Form, ...	10
Smoothness, ...	5
Naturalness of colored parts, .	5
Neatness of finish, . . .	. 5
Perfection, . . .	100

Single Bird Specimens.

Attitude, ...	15
Centre of gravity, .	15
Form, ...	. 15
Naturalness of size,	10
Smoothness, . . .	. 10
Angle of legs, .	10
Adjustment of wings, . .	10
Neatness of finish, . .	10
Naturalness of colored parts,	. 5
Perfection, . .	100

Groups of Reptiles and Fishes.

Smoothness, ...	. 15
Naturalness of size,	10
" of form, .	. 15
" of color, . .	15
Attitude, . .	. 10
Size and difficulty, . . ,	15
General neatness, .	5
General artistic effect, .	10
Quality of accessories,	. 5
Perfection, . .	100

Single Reptiles.

Smoothness, ...	. 15
Naturalness of size,	15
" of form, .	. 15
" of colors, .	15
Attitude, . . .	10
Size, ...	10
General difficulty,	. 10
" neatness, .	10
Perfection, .	100

Single Fishes.

Form, ...	. 20
Naturalness of size,	20
" of colors,	. 15
Smoothness, . . .	20
Style of mounting,	. 15
Expression, . .	5
Mouth-parts,	. 5
Perfection, .	. 100

Bird Skins (in collections.)

Naturalness of size, ...	. 15
Cleanliness, . .	15
Shape of head, . .	. 15
Position of wings, . .	15
Shape of neck, .	. 10
Position of legs, .	10
General form, .	. 10
Smoothness, . .	10
Perfection, .	. 100

Heads.

Size and difficulty, . . .	. 15
Form, . . .	15
Expression, . .	. 15
Smoothness, .	15
Mouth, . . .	. 10
Ears, ...	5
Naturalness of colored parts,	. 10
Style of mounting, . . .	10
General neatness, ...	5
Perfection,	. 100

CATALOGUE.

CLASS A.—TAXIDERMY PROPER.

Section 1.—Groups of Mammals.

1. "A Fight in the Tree-tops" (Orang outangs), Wm. T. Hornaday, . $800.00
   Loaned by Prof. H. A. Ward.
2. Gray Foxes,   David T. Bruce.

Section 2.—Groups of Birds.

No.
3. Cabinet Group (100 specimens), T. W. Fraine.
4. Game Birds (10 specimens),   T. W. Fraine,   .   .   . $60.00
5. Ruffed Grouse,   T. W. Fraine. Loaned by H. H. Warner.
6. Quails,   T. W. Fraine.   "   " H. H. Warner.
7. Snipe,   .   .   T. W. Fraine.   "   " H. H. Warner.
8. Woodcock and Young.   T. W. Fraine.   "   " H. H. Warner.
9. Woodcock,   .   .   .   T. W. Fraine.   - "   " H. H. Warner.
10. "A Mother's Care," (woodcock and young), T. W. Fraine.
11. Quails,   .   .   .   T. W. Fraine.
12. "The Cares of a Family," (Plovers), T. W. Fraine.
13. Quails,   .   T. W. Fraine.   Loaned by G. Bristow.
14. Quails,   .   .   .   T. W. Fraine.   "   " F. Bristow.
15. Australian Birds (10 specimens), T. W. Fraine.   "   " Mr. Busby.
16. Cabinet Group (10 specimens),   T. W. Fraine.
17. "A Wise Family" (Screech Owls), T. W. Fraine.
18. Group of Birds (7 specimens), Sam. F. Rathbun,   .   .   . $15.00
19. "Peace," (Owls),   .   Wm. G. Smith and Miss E. Smith.
20. Rails,   .   Wm. G. Smith and Miss E. Smith.
21. Plover,   .   .   .   Wm. G. Smith and Miss E. Smith.
22. Cabinet Case of Birds (54 spec.), Wm. G. Smith and Miss E. Smith.
23. Ducks,   .   .   .   Frank S. Wright,   .   . $50.00
24. Snowy Owls and Weasel,   .   Mr. and Mrs. G. H. Hedley,   35.00
25. Ruffled Grouse and Young,   .   Mr and Mrs. G. H. Hedley,   15.00
26. Sandpipers and Young,   .   Mr. and Mrs. G. H. Hedley,   15.00
27. Florida Gallinules,   .   Mr. and Mrs. G. H. Hedley,   12.00
28. Blue Jays,   .   Mr. and Mrs. G· H. Hedley,   .   12.00
29. Goshawks,   .   ,   Mr. and Mrs. G. H. Hedley,   25.00
30. Meadow Larks,   Mr. and Mrs. G. H. Hedley,   12.00
31. Green Herons,   .   Mr. and Mrs. G. H. Hedley,   12.00
32. Ruffle Head Ducks,   .   ,   Mr. and Mrs. G. H. Hedley,   12.00
33. Plover and Sandpipers,   Mr. and Mrs. G. H. Hedley,   12.00

No.

34.	Cedar Birds,	.	Mr. and Mrs. G. H. Hedley.	$ 12.00
35.	Blue Winged Teal,		Mr. and Mrs. G. H. Hedley,	25.00
36.	Scarlet Tanagers,	.	Mr. and Mrs. G. H. Hedley,	12.00
37.	Shore and Water Birds,		A. Myhill,	10.00
38.	Cabinet Group,	.	F. T. Jencks, .	150.00
39.	Group of Summer Birds (7 spec.), Geo. F. Hutchinson.			

40.	" Spring," (Blue-birds),	.	Frederic A. Lucas, .	$15.00	
41.	" Summer," (Yellow-birds), .		Frederic A. Lucas,	15.00	
42.	" Autumn," (Goldfinches),		Frederic A. Lucas, .	15.00	50.00
43.	" Winter," (Sparrows), .	.	Frederic A. Lucas,	15.00	

44.	" Winter," (Snow Buntings),	Frederic A. Lucas,	85.00
45.	" An Interrupted Dinner,"	Frederic A. Lucas,	85.00
46.	Summer Birds,	. . Henry L. Ward.	
47.	" A Mutual Surprise," (Ibis and Alligator), Wm. T. Hornaday,		25.00
48.	Game Birds of Monroe Co., N. Y.,	David T. Bruce.	
49.	Golden Eagle and Hare,	. . David T. Bruce.	
50.	Bald Eagle,	. . David T. Bruce.	
51.	Red-tailed Hawks,	David T. Bruce.	
52.	Goshawks,	. . David T. Bruce.	
53.	Snowy Owls, .	David T. Bruce,	
54.	Barred Owls,	David T. Bruce.	
55.	Hawk Owls,	. David T. Bruce.	
56.	Screech Owls,	David T. Bruce.	
57.	Prairie Hen, .	David T. Bruce.	
58.	Ruffed Grouse,	David T. Bruce.	
59.	Canada Grouse,	David T. Bruce.	
60.	Ptarmigan, . . .	David T. Bruce,	
61.	Snowy Owl and Bohemian Waxwing, David T. Bruce.		
62.	Canada Goose,	. David T. Bruce.	
63.	Woodcocks,	David T. Bruce.	
64.	Woodcocks,	David T. Bruce.	
65.	Woodcocks,	. David T. Bruce.	
66.	Snipe,	David T. Bruce.	
67.	Snipe, .	David T. Bruce.	
68.	Quail,	. David T. Bruce.	
69.	Quail, .	David T. Bruce.	
70.	Quail, . .	David T. Bruce.	
71.	California Quail,	David T. Bruce.	
72.	Yellow shanks,	David T. Bruce.	
73.	Green Herons, .	David T. Bruce.	
74.	Hooded Merganser,	David T. Bruce.	
75.	Wood Ducks,	David T. Bruce.	
76.	Wood Ducks,	David T. Bruce.	
77.	Goosander,	David T. Bruce.	
78.	Widgeons, .	David T. Bruce.	
79.	Long-tailed Ducks,	David T. Bruce.	
80.	Green-winged Teal.	David T. Bruce.	
81.	Blue-winged Teal,	David T. Bruce.	
82.	Buffle-Head Ducks,	David T. Bruce.	
83.	Sage Grouse, .	David T. Bruce.	

No.
84. Herring Gulls, . David T. Bruce.
85. Least Bittern, . . David T. Bruce.
86. Shore Birds (3 specimens), Dauid T. Bruce.
87. Great Northern Diver, David T. Bruce.
88. Sandpipers and Jacksnipe, David T. Bruce.
89. Wilson's Phalarope, . . David T. Bruce.
90. Yellow-billed Cuckoo and Bluebird, David T. Bruce.
91. "Summer," . E. L. Ormsbee.
92. "Winter," . . . . . E. L. Ormsbee.
93. "The Flamingo at Home," (8 spec.), F. S. Webster, . $200.00
94. "They are Mine," (Screech Owl and Young), F. S. Webster, 30.00
95. "Our Winter Friends," (Snow Buntings), , F. S. Webster, . 25.00
96. "The Falcon's Last Quarry," F. S. Webster, . . 10.00
97. "The Heronry" (Night Herons), F. S. Webster.
98. California Valley Quail, . T. T. Southwick.
99. California Mountain Quail, T. T. Southwick.

Section 3.—Groups of Reptiles.

Section 4.—Groups of Fishes.

100. "Fish for Dinner," C. E. De Kempeneer, $ 8.00
101. "A Morning's Catch," A. B. Baker, . . 5.00

Section 5.—Single Mammals.

102. Lion, . . J. Wallace.
103. Black Bear, . J. Wallace.
104. Tiger, . John Martens. Loaned by Prof. H. A. Ward, $175.00
105. Lioness, . John Martens. " " Prof. H. A. Ward, 110.00
106. Mountain Sheep, John Martens. " " Prof. H. A. Ward.
107. Prong-horn Antelope, John Martens. " " Prof. H. A. Ward.
108. Buffalo, John Martens. " " Prof. H. A. Ward, $150.00
109. Fur Seal, . . Wm. Critchley. Loaned by Prof. H. A. Ward, 75.00
110. Fur Seal (young), Wm. Critchley. " " Prof. H. A. Ward, 30.00
111. Civet Cat, . Wm. Critchley. " " Prof. H. A. Ward.
112. Albino Squirrel, T. W. Fraine. Loaned by G. W. Crouch, Jr.
113. Monkey, . E. L. Ormsbee.

Section 6.—Single Birds.

114. Bald Eagle, J. Wallace.
115. Golden Eagle, . J. Wallace.
116. Lammergeyer, F. S. Webster. Loaned by Prof. H. A. Ward.
117. Vulture, ... F. S. Webster. " " Prof. H. A. Ward.
118. Swallow-tailed Kite, . F. S. Webster. . . . $ 8.00
119. Golden Pheasant, . . F. S. Webster, 18.00
120. Wood Ibis (shot in N. Y.), F. S. Webster. . 10.00
121. Bonaparte's Gull, . F. S. Webster, . . 5,00
122. Melanite Red-headed Woodpecker, F. S. Webster, . 5.00

No.

123. Wood Duck,   F. S. Webster. Loaned by Prof H. A. Ward.
124. Owl, .   Wm. G. Smith and Miss E. Smith.
125. Hawks (2), . .   Wm. G. Smith and Miss E. Smith.
126. Crow,(under shade), .   Wm. G. Smith and Miss E. Smith.
127. Bittern, . .   Wm. G. Smith and Miss E. Smith.
128. Sea Gull, . . .   Wm. G. Smith and Miss E. Smith.
129. Woodcock, (under shade), Wm. G. Smith and Miss E. Smith.
130. Arctic Owl, . . . T. W. Fraine.
131. Spread Eagle (with national colors), T. W. Fraine.

                                                    Loaned by G. H. Ellwanger.
132. Scarlet Macaw, .   T. W. Fraine.   "   " Mr. Smith.
133. Blue Heron, .   T. W. Fraine.
134. English Pheasant,   T. W. Fraine.
135. Wood Duck, . T. W. Fraine.
136. Hawk (with prey), . T. W. Fraine.
137. Bald Eagle, "Old Chief," T. W. Fraine. Loaned by H. H. Warner.
138. Great Horned Owl, . T. W. Fraine.   "   " Dr. Porter Farley.
139. Arctic Owls (2),   T. W. Fraine.
140. Great Horned Owl.   T. W. Fraine.
141. Least Bittern, .   T. W. Fraine.
142. Green Heron,   T. W. Fraine.
143. Florida Heron,   T. W. Fraine. Loaned by Jas. Watson.
144. Screech Owl, .   J. F. D. Bailly, $2.50
145. African Gray Parrot. Nelson R. Wood.
146. King Lory, .   Nelson R. Wood,
147. Screech Owl, .   Nelson R. Wood.
148. Great Horned Owl,   A. B. Baker,   5.00

Section 7.—Single Reptiles.

149. Turtles,   Jules F. D. Bailly.

Section 8.—Single Fishes.

Section 9.—Heads.

150. Virginia Deer,   J. F. D. Bailly. Loaned by Prof. H. A. Ward.
151. Virginia Deer,   J. F. D. Bailly.   "   " F. A. Lucas.
152. Virginia Deer,   J. F. D. Bailly.
153. Virginia Deer, . A. B. Baker.
154. Virginia Deer,   T. W. Fraine.   "   " A. B. Lamberton.
155. Virginia Deer,   T. W. Fraine.   "   " Maj. Erbelding.
156. Virginia Deer,   T. W. Fraine.   "   " H. H. Warner.
157. Virginia Deer, . T. W. Fraine.   "   " Mr. Spaulding.
158. Virginia Deer,   T. W. Fraine.   "   " H. Smith.
159. Virginia Deer,   T. W. Fraine.   "   " H. Smith.
160. Virginia Deer,   T. W. Fraine.   "   " Mr. Kalbfleisch.
161. Virginia Deer,   T. W. Fraine.   "   " Mr. Howson.
162. Virginia Deer,   T. W. Fraine.   "   "
163. Virginia Deer,   T. W. Fraine.   "   " J. S. Watson.
164. Elk, .   T. W. Fraine.   "   " J. S. Watson.

No.
165. Pointer,   .   .   .   T. W. Fraine.
166. Monkey, "I should smile," F. A. Lucas, $12.00
167. Coyote, "On the Lookout," F. A. Lucas, ... $10.00
168. Tiger, (on rug),   .   Wm. T. Hornaday. Loaned by Mr. Geo. Upp.
169. Leopard, (on rug),   .   Wm. T. Hornaday. Louned by Mr. Geo. Upp.
170. Leopard, (on rug),   Wm. T. Hornaday. Loaned by Mr. Geo. Upp.
171. Leopard, (with rug),   Wm. T. Hornaday,   . $100.00
172. Virginia Deer,   .   John Wallace.

Section 10.—Skins.

173. Series of 150 Bird Skins.   W. E. D. Scott.
174. Lot of 16 Bird Skins.   Samuel F. Rathbun.
175. Lot of 25 Bird Skins.   Geo. F. Hutchison.
176. Lot of 12 Bird Skins.   Henry L. Ward.

Section 11.—Groups of Crustaceans.

177. "The Home of the Crab." (8 species).   C. E. DeKempeneer. $35.00

CLASS B.—NOVELTIES IN TAXIDERMY.

Section 1.—Grotesque Groups, and Animals Grotesquely Mounted.

178. "The Story of Cock Robin."   Complete.   Wm. G. and Miss E. Smith
179. "The Poacher,   .   Wm. G. and Miss E. Smith.
180. "A Chicken Dispute,"   Thos. W. Fraine.
181. Barred Owl,   . .   T. W. Fraine.
182. Long Eared Owl. .   T. W. Fraine.
183. Screech Owl. .   T. W. Fraine.
184. Screech Owl.   .   T. W. Fraine.
185. Saw-whet Owl.   . .   T. W. Fraine.
186. "Sitting for a Portrait." (Frogs.)   J. F. D. Bailly, $8.00
187. "Taking a Stroll," (Frog),   .   J. F. D. Bailly, $2.50
188. "The Taxidermist," (Frog),   .   J. F. D. Bailly, $4.00
189. "The Affair of Honor," (Frogs),   J. F. D. Bailly, $5.00
190. "Taking it Easy," (Frog),   .   J. F. D. Bailly, $3.00
191. "An Old Toper," (Frog),   .   J. F. D. Bailly,   . . $1.00
192. "The Lone Fisherman," (Frog),   J. F. D. Bailly.   Loaned.
193. "A Happy Family," (Frogs),   .   J. F. D. Bailly,   . $6.00
194. "Out in the Rain," (Frogs),   .   J. F. D. Bailly, $3.50
195. "Sold Again," (Frog),   .   J. F. D. Bailly, $4.00
196. "Taking a Walk," (Frog),   .   J. F. D. Bailly,   . . $2.50
197. "Boon Companions," (Frogs),   J. F. D. Bailly.   Loaned.
199. "The Long-horeman," (Frog),   J. F. D. Bailly, $2.50
199. "The Duel," (Squirrels),   .   J. F. D. Bailly, $5.00
200. "Domino!" (Squirrels),   J. F. D. Bailly, $5.50
201. "Euchred!" (Squirrels),   .   J. F. D. Bailly, $5.00
202. "Going to Church," (Squirrels),   J. F. D. Bailly,   . $5.00
203. "A Good Cigar," (Squirrels),   .   J. F. D. Bailly, $2.50
204. "The Lovers," (Kittens),   J. F. D. Bailly, $6.00
205. "The Violinist," (Crow),   J. F. D. Bailly,   . $5.00
206. "The Pedagogue," (Frog),   .   Wm. T. Hornaday.   Loaned.

207. " The Sick Child," (Frogs), . G. Mühl, . $2.75
208. " Practicing Gymnastics," (Frogs), G. Mühl, $4.00
209. " Young America," (Squirrel), G. Mühl, . $2.00

Section 2.--Articles of Use and Ornament.

210. Medallion, on easel (White Heron), F. S. Webster, . $40.00
211. Medallion, on easel (White Heron), F. S. Webster, . 40.00
212. Dead Game, (Ducks), Geo. F. Hutchison.
213. Dead Game, (Ducks), . Geo. F. Hutchison.
214. Medallion, (Orioles), . F. A. Lucas, ... 6.00
215. Panel Piece, (Eng. Pheasants), T. W. Fraine. Loaned by Mr. Thayer.
216. Panel Piece, (Blue Winged Teal),T. W. Fraine.
217. Panel Piece, (Teal), . . T. W. Fraine.
218. Panel Piece, (Partridge & Quail),T. W. Fraine. Loaned by C. C. Angle.
219. Panel Piece, (Mallard), . T. W. Fraine. " " C. H. Babcock.
220. Panel Piece, (Mallard), T. W. Fraine. " " "
221. Panel Piece, (Mallard), . T. W. Fraine. " " "
222. Panel Piece. (Mallard), . T. W. Fraine. " " "
223. Screen, (Peacock), . T. W. Fraine. Loaned by Mrs. P. M. Bromley.
224. Screen, (Peacock), . T. W. Fraine.
225. Screen, (Owl), . . T. W. Fraine.
226. Terrier Dog, on Rug, - T. W. Fraine.
227. Seal-skin Rug, . . . T. W. Fraine.
228. Case of Ladies' Hat-birds, Miss E. Smith.
229. Case of Ladies' Hat-birds, Miss E. Smith.
230. Watch Case, (Pigeon), . G. Mühl, . $3.00
231. Watch Case, (Pigeon), . G. Mühl, . . _ 3.00
232. Ottoman, (Elephant's Foot), . William Critchley.
Loaned by W. T. Hornaday.

CLASS C.—ADJUNCTS TO TAXIDERMY.

Section 1.—Taxidermist's Tools.

233. Geo. Tieman & Co., Cor. Chatham and Chambers Sts., N. Y. City.

Section 2.—Glass Eyes.

234. Demuth Brothers, . 89 Walker St., N. Y. City.
235. Christian Hahn, 16 N. William St., N. Y. City.

Section 3.—Artificial Leaves, Plants and Flowers.

236. Artificial Leaves, C. Pelletier, . . 135 Wooster St., N. Y. City.
237. Artificial Leaves, Maurice Gaupillot, . 51 Bleeker St., N. Y. City.

Section 4.—Rock Work.

Section 5.—Perches, &c.

238. Set of Bird Perches and Pedestals, Dr. Joseph B. Holder, American Museum, N. Y. City.
239. Set of Patent Perches, E. L. Ormsbee.

SECRETARY'S GENERAL REPORT.

MARCH 12th, 1880, TO MARCH 25th, 1881.

On Friday, March 12th, 1880, there met at No. 7 Elm Street, in the city of Rochester, F. S. WEBSTER, THOMAS W. FRAINE, FREDERIC A. LUCAS, JULES F. D. BAILLY, JOHN MARTENS, A. B. BAKER and WILLIAM T. HORNADAY, to discuss a plan for the formation of a national Society of Taxidermists. After a general discussion of the plan proposed, it was decided to undertake the formation of such a Society, and each gentleman present pledged himself to the support of the plan. Messrs. WEBSTER, LUCAS and HORNADAY were appointed a committee to draw up a Constitution, and a circular letter addressed to the taxidermists of this country.

At a meeting held on March 24th, the Society organized by electing the following officers :

President—FREDERIC S. WEBSTER.
Vice-President—THOMAS W. FRAINE.
Secretary—WILLIAM T. HORNADAY.
Treasurer—FREDERIC A. LUCAS.

A standing committee was appointed to act with the above officers. A Constitution was submitted and adopted, and five hundred copies ordered printed for general distribution. A circular letter was submitted, approved, and three hundred copies were ordered printed. The Secretary was instructed to send a copy of the Constitution and the circular letter to every taxidermist in this country whose name and address could be obtained. About one hundred and sixty copies of these documents were sent out, and in reply to this extended invitation only two persons responded at once, GEORGE H. HEDLEY, of Medina, and A. H. WOOD. of Painted Post. Both these gentlemen joined the Society, and were the first out-of-town members secured. The Society held a business meeting on the first Friday in each month, in the rooms of the Monroe County Sportsmen's Club, in the city of Rochester, which had been kindly placed at the disposal of the Society.

A number of prominent scientists and patrons of taxidermy were elected honorary members of the Society, and their letters of sympathy and encouragement had great influence with outsiders in inducing them to join the organization. F. T. JENCKS, of Providence became a member at the August meeting, and Professor W. E. D. SCOTT, of Princeton, N. J., in September, which added very materially to the prestige of the Society, and was the means of bringing in several valuable working members.

It was at first proposed to hold the first annual exhibition in September, but it was finally postponed to the third week in December, in order to allow more time to prepare exhibits. Early in November, Mr. JAMES VICK offered the Society, rent free, an elegant and commodious hall for use during the exhibition, which generous act gave a fresh impulse to the plans of the Society. Three weeks before the date set for the opening of the exhibition, DAVID T. BRUCE, of Brockport, joined the Society, and promised to furnish a large exhibit, which promise has been grandly fulfilled, although at great expense and trouble.

When it was finally apparent that the exhibition would be one of which we need not feel ashamed, it was decided to try and induce prominent eastern men to be present and act as judges, and, to the satisfaction of the Society and all its friends, Professor J. A. ALLEN, of Cambridge, Dr. JOSEPH B. HOLDER, of New York, and Professor W. E. D. SCOTT, of Princeton, consented to be present and act as a judges' committee.

The exhibition hall was in every respect all that could be desired, being 120 feet in length by 30 in width, well lighted, easy of access, and centrally located. With but one or two slight exceptions, all the exhibits were in place and the arrangement of the exhibition complete on Monday, December 13th. On the day following the judges had sole possession of the hall, and the day was spent in examining the objects entered in competition for prizes. No exhibitors' names appeared upon any of the objects, but each object entered in competition was marked by a number and the letter of the alphabet which had been assigned to the exhibitor.

The exhibition was formally opened on Tuesday evening, December 14th, by a reception, for which about three hundred and fifty cards of invitation were issued. The attendance was in every respect a high compliment to the Society. Every object displayed was fully labeled with catalogue number, class, section, title, and exhibitor's name and address. It is worthy of record that the public expression of surprise at the extent and variety of the display was universal.

The exhibition opened to the general public on December 15th, to continue daily from 10 A. M. to 10 P. M. until the 18th, inclusive. In order to meet the expenses of the exhibition, an admission fee of twenty-five cents was charged. Owing to the increasing attendance and the interest manifested by the public up to the time originally set for closing the exhibition, the Executive Committee deemed it both necessary and advisable to continue the exhibition three days longer. By full consent of the proprietors of the hall, this was done, and the first annual exhibition finally closed on Wednesday, December 22d, at 10 P. M.

For the success of the first exhibition, the Society is greatly indebted to the daily press of this city, particularly the *Rochester Democrat and Chronicle* and the *Morning Herald*, which, by extended reports and numerous local notices, drew public attention to the Society and its work. In view of the fact that the exhibitions of this Society are of a character entirely new to the public, and their various features of interest are as yet unknown and therefore unappreciated, the good offices of the press generally are at present an important factor in the financial success of the Society's undertakings. The Society asks only a fair introduction to public favor, and desires to stand strictly upon its merits. It will ever bear in grateful remembrance the liberal and kindly efforts of the Rochester daily press to encourage and strengthen a new undertaking, and which contributed so largely to the financial success of the first display made by the Society.

The first general meeting of the Society was held on Wednesday, December 15, at 2 P.M., in the rooms of the Monroe County Sportsmen's Club, 128 Reynolds' Arcade. The meeting was called to order, and President WEBSTER read an address upon the history of taxidermy.

Owing to the unusual amount of labor required upon matters pertaining to the holding of a first exhibition, only one paper had been prepared to be read before the Society, and under the circumstances it was thought best to have it held over until the next meeting, when a more general effort will be made in this line of the Society's work.

At the close of President WEBSTER'S address, the Society went into committee of the whole on the revision of the Constitution. By vote of three-fourths of the members present, the following changes in the Constitution were made : Articles 2, 3, 4, 6, 8, 10, 11, 13, 14, 15, 16, 17 and 18 were amended in various ways by substitutions or striking out. Article 5 was stricken out entirely, and also section 2 of Article 14. A new article was introduced between Articles 12 and 13, and four new sections, numbered 5, 6, 7 and 8 respectively, were added to Article 13. The Constitution as amended was ordered printed and distributed, to take the place of the original document.

The names of three candidates for membership were presented as follows : Rev. WILLIAM ELGIN, of Rochester ; DAVID T. BRUCE, Jr., of Brockport ; and CHAS. H. HEDLEY, of Medina. A ballot was taken, and the above named gentlemen were declared elected.

Dr. JOSEPH B. HOLDER, of New York, was nominated for election as an honorary member. and was elected by acclamation.

The following resolutions were offered and adopted as read :

Offered by Mr. WILLIAM T. HORNADAY :

Resolved, That the thanks of the Society be tendered the eminent gentlemen who, at the sacrifice of their valuable time and personal convenience, have consented to honor the Society by being present at this exhibition and acting as judges of the same, by which they have shown the public their interest in the Society and rendered invaluable assistance in establishing it upon a permanent basis.

Offered by Mr. THOMAS W. FRAINE :

Resolved, That the thanks of the Society be tendered Mr. JAMES VICK for his extreme kindness in placing an elegant and commodious hall at the disposal of the Society, rent free, during its first annual exhibition, and thereby contributing so important an element toward the success of the same.

Offered by Mr. WILLIAM G. SMITH :

Resolved, That the thanks of the Society be tendered Messrs. JOHN FAHY & Co. for their generosity in allowing the Society to occupy, during the third week in December, the premises which have recently passed into their hands, and which favor they granted the Society at the sacrifice of their own plans and convenience.

Offered by Mr. JAMES S. WATSON :

Resolved, That the thanks of the Society be tendered the Hon. ALFRED ELY, for his kindness in consenting to allow the Society to occupy with its exhibition the hall which had been offered conditionally by JAMES VICK.

Offered by Mr. T. T. SOUTHWICK :

Resolved, That the thanks of the Society be tendered the Monroe County Sportsmen's Club, for its courtesy and kindness in granting this Society the use of its elegant club room for the holding of our meetings during the past year.

Offered by Mr. FREDERIC A. LUCAS:

Resolved, That the thanks of the Society are due, and are hereby tendered the *Rochester Democrat and Chronicle, Morning Herald, Evening Express*, and the *Union and Advertiser*, for their liberal reports and local notices of the Society and its exhibition.

On motion and second, the Society appointed Messrs. WEBSTER, LUCAS and N. R. WOOD to act as judges upon the bird skins and accessories to taxidermy displayed in the exhibition.

The appointment of the time and place for the holding of the next general meeting and exhibition, was deferred until the first quarterly business meeting of the ensuing year.

The election of officers for the coming year was held, and resulted as follows :

President—Prof. W. E. D. SCOTT, of Princeton, N. J.

Vice President—FREDERIC S. WEBSTER, of Rochester, N. Y.

Secretary—WILLIAM T. HORNADAY, of Rochester, N. Y.

Treasurer—FREDERIC A. LUCAS, of Rochester, N. Y.

Executive Committee -THOMAS W. FRAINE, WILLIAM G. SMITH, and J. F. D. BAILLY, of Rochester, N. Y.

On motion the meeting adjourned, subject to the call of the President.

The Report of the Judges was opened and read to the members of the Society in the exhibition hall, on Friday evening, December 17th.

The first quarterly business meeting of the Society for the year 1881 was held in Rochester, on Friday, March 25th, at 8 P. M. President SCOTT presided over the meeting. Eight new members were elected. The names of three delinquents were dropped, and two members resigned on account of lack of time to devote to taxidermic work. A committee, appointed at the general meeting, consisting of Messrs. SCOTT, LUCAS, WEBSTER, SOUTHWICK and WATSON, reported on the revision of Article 13 of the Constitution, and the report submitted was adopted, with but one amendment.

A list of special honors proposed by the Executive Committee, to be awarded at the next exhibition, was read before the Society, approved, and ordered printed in the report.

The reports of the Secretary and Treasurer, up to date, were read, and ordered printed.

The Executive Committee nominated Boston as the best place in which to hold the next general meeting and exhibition, and the date recommended was November 28th to December 7th. On motion and second, it was decided that the Second Annual Meeting and Exhibition shall be held in Boston, at such a date as may be fixed hereafter by the Executive Committee.

The President appointed a Local Committee, after which the meeting adjourned.

Respectfully submitted,

WM. T. HORNADAY,
Secretary.

COMMUNICATIONS.

The foliowing communications are submitted as being of general interest.

WM. T. HORNADAY, Sec'y.

DEPARTMENT OF THE INTERIOR,
FISHERIES DIVISION, NEWPORT, R. I.,
August 6th, 1880.

DEAR SIR : It gives me great pleasure to accept the election to honorary membership in the Society of American Taxidermists. I sympathize heartily with the members of the Society in their desire to raise the art of taxidermy in America to the highest standard of excellence. In the late Fishery Exhibition in Berlin much of the taxidermy in the American exhibit, both in the display of the National Museum and that of Professor Ward, was fully equal to the best examples to be found in the Museum at Berlin. I am sure that such a society as the one you have founded will do much towards stimulating study and experiment, and that by its means mechanical and artistic perfection in work of this class will be more nearly approximated than ever in the past.

Yours, very respectfully,

G. BROWN GOODE.

Mr. Wm. T. Hornaday, Secretary of the Society of American Taxidermists, Rochester, N. Y.

MUSEUM OF COMPARATIVE ZOOLOGY,
CAMBRIDGE, Mass., June 28, 1880.

William T. Hornaday, Secretary Society of American Taxidermists :

MY DEAR SIR : In accepting an honorary membership of the Society of American Taxidermists, which your official letter of the 25th informs me the Society has tendered me, I must first state that I make no claim to skill in the art of taxidermy, and for this reason have perhaps no right to the honor bestowed. * * * I appreciate good work in taxidermy, and am aware of the difficulties that stand in the way of success, and therefore shall be most happy to aid in any way in my power to elevate this art to a permanent and acknowledged position among the fine arts. one of which, in its possibilities and the skill it requires, it really is.

The plan of operations laid down in the Constitution of the Society, it appears to me, if seconded by taxidermists at large, as it is to be hoped it will be, must stimulate effort toward the attainment of a high standard of excellence, and thus result in great good.

Heartily wishing you success in your praiseworthy enterprise, I remain,

Very faithfully yours,

J. A. ALLEN.

18

WARD'S NATURAL SCIENCE ESTABLISHMENT, ⎱
ROCHESTER, N.Y., June 24, 1880. ⎰

Wm. T. Hornaday, Secretary of the Society American Taxidermists :

DEAR SIR : Your letter of the 10th inst. came duly to hand on my return from abroad last week. It pleased me to be informed that your Society has done me the honor to invite me to a position in it as an honorary member. I am gratified to know that you have formed a society for the avowed purpose of elevating the standard of work in taxidermy and raising it to the position it should hold among other fine arts. This is truly a purpose worthy of all success.

I believe that by a few years of earnest work, with the incentive thereto which it supplies, your Society can cause a great and permanent advance in the art of taxidermy, conferring a solid boon on the science of zoology, besides winning for yourselves an enviable reputation as artists.

I deem it a pleasure to accept the position which you have so courteously tendered me, and I will gladly assist you in carrying out your plans whenever I can properly do so. I hope that your spirit and enterprise will in the end be crowned with brilliant success.

Yours very truly,

HENRY A. WARD.

MUSEUM OF NATURAL HISTORY, ⎱
COLLEGE OF CHARLESTON, S. C., ⎰
27th June, 1880.

William T. Hornaday. Secretary S. A. T. :

MY DEAR SIR : I have the honor of acknowledging the reception of your favor inviting me to become an honorary member of your Society. It gives me great pleasure to be thus identified with an association the objects of which I so thoroughly sympathize with, and I hereby accept the position you offer me.

It has often been a source of wonder to me that the art of taxidermy should not occupy a higher level with us in America. It is so often associated with other occupations that I presume its dignity has been thus somewhat lowered. There is no reason, however, why the taxidermist should not hold his head as high as any man. He is eminently a student of nature, and when, as a result of his observation and skill, he is able to produce a counterpart of life itself, he is entitled to rank on the same level as the painter or the sculptor.

Your Society is one that has my heartiest endorsement, and it is particularly gratifying to me, who am in constant intercourse with members of that calling, to be considered one of their well-wishers.

I remain, my dear sir, with great respect.

Faithfully yours, G. E. MANIGAULT.

AMERICAN MUSEUM OF NATURAL HISTORY, ⎱
CENTRAL PARK, NEW YORK, December 22d, 1880. ⎰

Wm. T. Hornaday, Secretary of the Society of American Taxidermists :

MY DEAR SIR : Your very kindly letter is at hand, wherein you inform me that the Society of American Taxidermists, at their late general meeting, unanimously elected me an honorary member thereof.

Please convey to your Society my high appreciation of the honor. I receive it as such, and desire always to be in the front rank when its welfare and the highest attainment of its purposes can be aided by me,

Very truly yours, J. B. HOLDER.

TREASURER'S REPORT.

MARCH 24th, 1880, TO MARCH 25th, 1881.

To the Executive Committee of the S. A. T.:

SIRS.—I have the honor to submit the accompanying brief statement of the financial condition of the Society. The balance now in the treasury is small ; but the Society is free from debt. It is not too much to say that for this the Society is almost wholly indebted to Mr. JAMES VICK, whose kindness in placing at its disposal the hall in which the Exhibition was held assured the financial success of the display. The Monroe County Sportsman's Club kindly declined to charge for the use of the room in which the monthly meetings were held, and the papers and Street Car Company gave lowest advertising rates. To the *Democrat and Chronicle* and *Daily Herald* the Society is especially indebted for very full and frequent notices. To PROFESSOR WARD our thanks are due not only for bearing a large share of the expenses of our judges, but in numerous other ways. Also to PROF. SCOTT, who, although one of the judges, bore his own expenses. Nor would it be just to pass over in silence those members, and those of our friends, especially those ladies, who contributed so much valuable time and assistance toward the preparation of the hall in which the exhibition was held. Personally I wish to express thanks to Messrs. WEBSTER, HORNADAY and BAILLY for advancing funds to meet the preliminary expenses of the display. In preparing for another exhibition. the Society should bear in mind that, while it is not at all probable that it will receive so much outside aid as in the past, the outlay will be much greater. At the same time if the best interests of the Society are to be advanced it seems almost indispensable that the next exhibition should be held outside of Rochester, lest the Society should come to be regarded as a merely local one, and thus suffer by an over-prudent economy. I therefore trust that as the time for the exhibition draws near we shall find members who are willing to incur a little risk for the credit of the Society.

Respectfully submitted,

FREDERIC A. LUCAS,

Treasurer.

SOCIETY OF AMERICAN TAXIDERMISTS.

Summary of Accounts.

RECEIPTS.

Entrance Receipts at Exhibition....	$286.72
Ten per cent. on sales	24.25
Admission fees, etc.	125.55
	$436.52

EXPENDITURES.

Heating Exhibition Hall....	$26.00
Lighting Exhibition Hall	20.02
Use of Gas Fixtures................., ...	15.70
Janitor's fees...................	15.00
Expenses of Judges	32.25
Door-keeper and attendants	47.20
Advertising	34.36
Printing tickets, diplomas, etc....	85.75
Stationary and Postage	20.43
Medals.............	22.25
150 blank Diplomas	25.00
Sundry small expenses	88.21
	$432.17
Balance in Treasury............................	$4.35

Assets and Liabilities of the Society.

ASSETS.

Money in Treasury..................................	$4.35
Cartages	1.50
Entrance fees and annual dues	70.00
	$75.85

LIABILITIES.

Photographic work	$14.00
Members who will withdraw	4.00
Doubtful receipts......	7.00
Engrossing Diplomas	6.50
Expenses of President	25.00
	$56.50
Balance in favor of Society.	19.35

The above accounts have been audited, and by the vouchers for the same, are found to be correct.

J. F. D. BAILLY,   } *Auditors.*
JOHN MARTENS,

A Fight in the Tree-Tops.

GROUP BY WM. T. HORNADAY.

Report of Judges' Committee

AND

List of Awards.

The judges appointed by the Society of American Taxidermists for their first Annual Exhibition, December 14th to 18th, 1880, have the honor to report the following awards:

I. For the best piece in the entire exhibition, Silver Medal.

This award is made to WM. T. HORNADAY for a group of mammals entitled "A Fight in the Tree-tops."

II. For the second best piece in the entire exhibition, Bronze Medal.

This award is made to FREDERIC S. WEBSTER for a single bird marked in the catalogue No. 123, "Wood Duck."

III. For the best general exhibit, Bronze Medal.

This award is made to JOHN MARTENS for pieces No. 104, Tiger; No. 105, Lioness; No. 106, Mountain Sheep; No. 107, Prong-horned Antelope; No. 108, Buffalo;—five pieces, having an average excellence of 84 points.

IV. For the second best general exhibit, Diploma of Honor.

Awarded to F. S. WEBSTER. This consists of nine pieces, marked 93, 94, 95, 96, 116, 117, 118, 119, 123, which average 77 points.

V. To each exhibit in Class A, Taxidermy Proper, standing at or over 85 points, a Diploma of Honor.

1. To exhibit No. 110, Young Fur Seal, by WM. CRITCHLEY. This piece is adjudged at 85 points in excellence.

2. To exhibit No. 165, Head of a Pointer Dog, by THOMAS W. FRAINE. This piece is marked by the judges 90 points in excellence.

3. To exhibit 101, Fishes, entitled "A Morning's Catch," by A. B. BAKER. This piece is marked by the judges 85 points in excellence.

VI. To each exhibit in Class A, standing at 75 points and under 85, a Certificate of Merit.

1. To exhibit 45, a group of birds entitled, "An Interrupted Dinner," by FRED A. LUCAS. This piece is marked at 75 points in excellence.

2. To exhibit 163, a Deer's Head by T. W. FRAINE. Marked at 75 points.

3. To exhibit 132, a single bird, Scarlet Macaw, by T. W. Fraine. Marked at 75 points.

4. To exhibit 150, Deer's Head, by J. F. D. BAILLY. Marked 80 points.

5. To exhibit 102, Lion, by JOHN WALLACE. Marked 75 points.

6. To exhibit 106, entitled "I Should Smile," by FRED A. LUCAS. Marked 75 points.

7. To exhibit 55, group of birds, by DAVID T. BRUCE. Marked 75 points.

8. To exhibit 58, cabinet group of birds, by F. T. JENCKS. Marked 75 points.

9. To exhibit 100, group of fish, by C. E. DEKEMPENEER.

VII. For Grotesque Groups and Animals Grotesquely Mounted.

1. A Diploma of Honor to J. F. D. BAILLY.

2. A Certificate of Merit to MISS E. and MR. WM. G. SMITH.

3. A Certificate of Merit to GEORGE MÜHL.

VIII. For the handsomest articles of ornament or use, a Diploma of Honor.

1. To F. S. WEBSTER, for Medallions, (White Herons).

IX. For second handsomest article of ornament or use, a Certificate of Merit.

1. To T. W. FRAINE, for Fire Screen, No. 223, Peacock).

Respectfully submitted,

J. A. ALLEN,
J. B. HOLDER,
W. E. D. SCOTT,
Judges.

LIST OF AWARDS GRANTED BY THE SOCIETY ALONE,

ROCHESTER, N. Y., Dec. 22d, 1880.

The judges appointed by the Society to report upon the exhibits of Bird Skins, and Accessories to Taxidermy, have the honor to report the following awards :

Class A, Section 10. Bird Skins.

The exhibit of PROF. SCOTT was withheld from competition.
To S. F. RATHBUN, Auburn, N. Y., Certificate of Merit.
To GEO. F. HUTCHINSON, Rochester, N. Y., Certificate of Merit.

Class C, Section 1. Taxidermists' Tools.

To GEO. TIEMAN & Co., Chatham Street, N. Y., Diploma of Honor.

Class C, Section 2. Glass Eyes.

To CHRISTIAN HAHN, 16 N. William St., N. Y., Certificate of Merit.

Class C, Section 3. Artificial Leaves.

1. To MAURICE GAUPILLOT, 51 Bleeker St., N. Y., Diploma of Honor.
2. To C. PELLETIER, 135 Wooster St., N. Y., Certificate of Merit.

Class C, Section 5. Perches.

To E. L. ORMSBEE, Cleveland, Ohio, Certificate of Merit.

Respectfully Submitted,

F. S. WEBSTER,
F. A. LUCAS,
NELSON R. WOOD,
Judges.

CONSTITUTION

OF THE

SOCIETY OF AMERICAN TAXIDERMISTS.

NAME.

ARTICLE 1.   This body shall be known as the SOCIETY OF AMERICAN TAXIDERMISTS.

OBJECTS.

ARTICLE 2.   The objects of this Society are to promote intercourse between those who are interested in the art of Taxidermy in various parts of America, to encourage and promote the development of that art, and to elevate it to a permanent and acknowledged position among the fine arts.

MEMBERSHIP.

ARTICLE 3.   Any taxidermist, whether amateur or professional, may become a member of the Society upon the written recommendation of one member, nomination by the Executive Committee, and election by a majority of members present at any regular meeting.

ARTICLE 4.   The Society shall consist of Active members, Corresponding members, and Honorary members.

OFFICERS.

ARTICLE 5.   The officers of the Society shall be elected by ballot in general session, and shall consist of a President, Vice President, Secretary and Treasurer, each of whom shall be elected at each annual meeting for the following one.

ARTICLE 6.   The President, or in his absence the Vice President, shall preside at all general sessions of the Society, and at all meetings of the Executive Committee.

It shall be the duty of the President to give an address at a general meeting of the Society during the meeting over which he shall preside.

ARTICLE 7. The Secretary shall be the executive officer of the Society under the direction of the Executive Committee. He shall keep an account of all business that he transacts for the Society, and make an annual report which shall be laid before the Society. He shall issue a circular of information to members at least two months before each meeting, and shall in connection with the Executive and Local Committees, make all necessary arrangements for the meetings and exhibitions of the Society. He shall receive and bring before the Executive Committee the titles and abstracts of papers proposed to be read before the Society. He shall receive and hold in trust for the Society all books, pamphlets, and manuscripts belonging to the association and allow the use of the same under the direction of the Executive Committee. He shall receive all communications addressed to the Society during the interval between meetings, and properly attend to the same.

ARTICLE 8. The Treasurer shall collect all assessments and admission fees and notify members of any arrearages. He shall keep an account of all receipts and expenditures of the Society, and make an annual report of the same to the Executive Committee for publication.

ARTICLE 9. The Executive Committee shall consist of the President, Vice-President, Secretary and Treasurer, and three members elected by ballot in general session. The duties of the Executive Committee shall be to manage the financial affairs of the Society ; to nominate members ; to arrange the business and programmes for general session ; to appoint general sessions ; to nominate the general officers for the following year, and to act upon all invitations extended to the Society ; to examine papers and decide which shall be read and published in the proceedings. The Executive Committee shall meet at the call of the President.

ARTICLE 10. The Local Committee shall consist of members of the Society, residing at or near the place of the proposed meeting. It is expected that the Local Committee, assisted by the officers of the Society, will make all essential arrangements for the meeting, and issue a circular giving necessary particulars at least two weeks before the meeting.

MEETINGS AND EXHIBITIONS.

ARTICLE 11. There shall be every year, at such time and place as the Executive Committee may nominate and be chosen by a majority of the members, a general meeting of the Society and an exhibition of work, for four days or longer. General sessions shall be held at 10 o'clock A. M., unless otherwise ordered, on every day of the meeting, Sundays excepted, at which time papers may be read and discussed.

ARTICLE 12. Besides the general meeting, the President and Executive Committee shall have the power to call a business meeting of the Society, once every three months if necessary, in the town or city which contains the largest number of Society officers or active members.

ARTICLE 13. *Section 1.* Every exhibition shall be competitive throughout, and will be divided into four classes, viz : Mammals, Birds, Reptiles and Fishes. In each of these classes there shall be awarded a CERTIFICATE OF MERIT, showing that any one holding such certificate has made a highly creditable exhibit of mounted specimens in that section. The Certificate of Merit shall be equivalent to a second class prize, but when two or more exhibits are of equal merit, then each one shall be awarded a certificate.

Section 2. In each class there shall also be awarded a DIPLOMA OF HONOR, showing that any one holding such diploma has made a first class exhibit in that class.

The Diploma of Honor shall be equivalent to a first prize, but more than one may be awarded in each class under the same conditions as the certificate.

Section 3. There shall be a SILVER MEDAL awarded to any member of the Society who shall win a Diploma of Honor in each of the four different classes, whether at one exhibition or at many, or to any member who shall at any one exhibition make a first class exhibit of specimens in each of the four classes—Mammals, Birds, Reptiles and Fishes. This shall be known as the MEDAL FOR GENERAL AVERAGE.

Section 4. There shall be a SILVER MEDAL awarded at each exhibition for the best special piece of work which shall reveal the most artistic design, the most perfect execution and the greatest amount of surmounted difficulty. In case there should be in any one exhibition two or more pieces of work, differing in character but of equal excellence, then more than one silver medal may be awarded at a single exhibition. Such medal shall be known as the SPECIALTY MEDAL.

Section 5. There shall be awarded at each annual exhibition, for the second best piece of work, in whichever of the four classes such work may appear, a BRONZE MEDAL. This medal shall be known as the SECOND SPECIALTY MEDAL.

Section 6. The Executive Committee shall present to the Society, six months before each annual exhibition, a schedule of awards embracing those already detailed in this article (13), and such additional special classes to be awarded medals, diplomas or certificates, as the committee deem expedient. On the approval of a majority of the Society this schedule shall form the basis of award at the ensuing annual exhibition, and each member of the Society shall at once be furnished with such approved schedule on which awards are to be made.

Section 7. A committee of three, to be called the Inspection Committee, shall be appointed by the Executive Committee, at such time as shall be deemed proper, before each annual exhibition. This committee shall have the power to report to the Standing Committee on the condition of the exhibits entered. Exhibitors shall send their names and addresses to the chairman of the committee, together with a list of the objects they intend to enter.

Section 8. The judges who shall award prizes must be furnished by the Secretary with a printed copy of Article 13, and the accepted schedule of the Executive Committee.

ARTICLE 14. *Section 1.* No piece having taken a prize shall be entered for competition a second time, but such piece may be placed on exhibition as often as its proprietor desires.

Section 2. No member shall ever exhibit any specimens other than those mounted by his own hands, under penalty of expulsion from the Society and forfeiture of all honors previously won. Upon entering specimens for any exhibition, every exhibitor shall sign a written declaration that said specimens have been mounted by his own hands, and without skilled assistance of any kind from any other taxidermist.

JUDGES.

ARTICLE 15. For each exhibition there shall be elected by the Society three competent judges, who are not active members, who shall critically examine each specimen, group, or collection which is entered in competition in the exhibition, and award it the honor to which it is justly entitled. The decisions and awards of the judges shall be final.

PAPERS AND COMMUNICATIONS.

ARTICLE 16. All members must forward to the Secretary as early as possible before the convening of the Society, full titles of the papers they propose to present during the meeting, with a statement of the time that each will occupy in delivery, and also such abstracts of their contents as will give a general idea of their nature.

PRINTED REPORT.

ARTICLE 17. The Secretary shall have a full report of each general meeting and exhibition printed in an octavo volume as soon after the meeting as possible. Authors must prepare their papers ready for press within one month after adjournment, otherwise only the abstracts will appear in the printed volumes. Illustrations must be provided for by the authors of the papers, or by a special appropriation from the Executive Committee. Whenever a silver medal is awarded for a special piece of work, whether a single specimen or a group, said piece of work shall be photographed at the expense of the Society, and a copy of the same inserted as a frontispiece to the volume of the report for that meeting and exhibition. Immediately on publication of the volume, a copy shall be forwarded to every member of the Society who shall not be in arrears upon the Treasurer's books, and it shall also be offered for sale by the Secretary. The Executive Committee shall designate the institutions to which copies shall be distributed.

ADMISSION FEE AND ASSESSMENT.

ARTICLE 18. The admission fee for active members shall be three dollars. The annual assessment for active members shall be two dollars, payable within one year under penalty of expulsion from the Society.

All fees and assessments must be paid to the Treasurer who shall give proper receipts for the same.

ARTICLE 19. The accounts of the Treasurer shall be audited annually by two auditors appointed by the President.

AMENDMENTS OF THE CONSTITUTION.

ARTICLE 20. No part of this Constitution shall be amended or annulled without the concurrence of three-fourths of the members, either present in general session, or voting by postal card to the Secretary.

Society of American Taxidermists.

LIST OF OFFICERS FOR 1881.

PRESIDENT.

PROF. W. E. D. SCOTT, - - - - - - - of Princeton, N. J.

VICE PRESIDENT.

FREDERIC S. WEBSTER, - - - - - - of Rochester, N. Y.

SECRETARY.

WM. T. HORNADAY, - - - - - - - of Rochester, N. Y.

TREASURER.

FREDERIC A. LUCAS, - - - - - - - of Rochester, N. Y.

EXECUTIVE COMMITTEE.

THOS W. FRAINE, - - - - - - - of Rochester, N. Y.
WM. G. SMITH, - - - - - - - - of Rochester, N. Y.
JULES F. D. BAILLY, - - - - - - - of Rochester, N. Y.
And the above General Officers.

LOCAL COMMITTEE FOR THE BOSTON MEETING AND EXHIBITION.

NEWTON DEXTER, Chairman, - - - - - of Providence, R. I.
F. T. JENCKS, - - - - - - - - of Providence, R. I.
PERCY W. ALDRICH, - - - - - - - of Boston, Mass.
FREDERIC A. LUCAS, - - - - - - of Rochester, N. Y.
CHAS. M. CARPENTER, - - - - - - of Providence, R. I.
GEO. M. GRAY, - - - - - - - - of Providence, R. I.

LIST OF HONORS, REGULAR AND SPECIAL, TO BE AWARDED AT THE BOSTON EXHIBITION,

To be held on or about November 28th to December 7th, 1881.

REGULAR PRIZES,

Provided for Annually by the Constitution.

For the best piece in entire exhibition, - - Specialty Medal, (Silver).
For the second best piece in the entire exhibition, Second Specialty Medal,(Bronze).
For the best general exhibit according to Article
    13, Section 3, of the Constitution, - - General Average Medal, (Silver).
To each exhibit in Class A, Taxidermy Proper, as
    per exhibition catalogue, which shall stand
    at 85 per cent. or over, - - - - Diploma of Honor.
To each exhibit in Class A which shall stand at
    75 and under 85 per cent., - - - Certificate of Merit.

SPECIAL PRIZES.

List compiled and approved by the Executive Committee.

For the best miscellaneous exhibit which, in the opinion of the
    judges, presents, *as a whole,* the most creditable appear-
    ance, - - - - - - - - - - Bronze Medal.
For the best exhibit of Reptiles, - - - - - Bronze Medal.
For the best exhibit of Fishes, - - - - - - Bronze Medal.
For the best collection of heads, size and quality considered, Silver Medal.
For the best display of articles of ornament or use. - - Silver Medal.
For the handsomest article of ornament or use, - - - Diploma of Honor.
For the second handsomest article of ornament or use, - Certificate of Merit.
For the best exhibit of grotesque groups and animals grotes-
    quely mounted, - - - - - - - - Bronze Medal.
For grotesque groups, etc., Diplomas and Certificates will be
    awarded at the discretion of the judges.
For the best exhibit of Accessories to Taxidermy, in each
    section, - - - - - - - - - Diploma of Honor.
For the second best in the same, - - - - - Certificate of Merit.

It is to be understood that the judges have the power to withhold any one of the above Special Prizes, if it shall ever occur that the exhibit ranking "best" or "second best" shall be deemed unworthy of an award.

By order of the Standing Committee.

WM. T. HORNADAY, *Sec'y.*

GROUP BY FREDERIC S. WEBSTER.

ADDRESS

OF

PRESIDENT WEBSTER.

FIRST GENERAL MEETING, DECEMBER 15th, 1880.

Ladies and Gentlemen of the Society of American Taxidermists:

I truly wish that the subject upon which I am called to speak was in abler hands. At this time, when the eyes of men of science and devotees of art are directed toward us ; when skeptics are waiting to hear the verdict, "Success " or " Failure," I feel that I am unequal to the exigencies of the hour. In view of the fact that this organization is the first of its kind, and that until now no systematic effort has been made to advance the art of taxidermy, it is fitting that we should enter into a brief retrospect and see what our art has been in the past.

A thorough history of taxidermy has never been written. A few scattering accounts have been recorded from time to time, but never a concise record ; therefore I can procure no authentic account of the time when this art was first practiced as such. Indeed, it is doubtful if before the seventeenth century it could have been considered an art. The word taxidermy is derived from the Greek words, "$\tau\alpha\xi\iota\varsigma$," arrangement, and " $\delta\epsilon\rho\pi\alpha$," skin, and is the name applied to the art of preserving and mounting, in a life-like manner, the skins of vertebrate animals.

In Johnson's Encyclopœdia we find the following interesting account written by one of the distinguished gentlemen who has honored this Society by acting as one of the judges of our first exhibition. Dr. J. B. HOLDER writes as follows of Taxidermy :

"In the year 1828 an Englishman named SCHUDDER established a museum in the ' Old Almshouse,' on Chambers Street, New York, where he prepared in the rude manner of the time, birds and quadrupeds. CHARLES WATERTON did much to elevate taxidermy to a high position, and through the genius of TITIAN R. PEALE the art in this country improved. The late JULES VERREAUX, of Paris, brought it to a degree of perfection that fairly rivals some of the examples of the higher plastic arts."

Leaving the date of the employment of the art in America, let us consider the advent of taxidermy in foreign countries. It is uncertain what degree of perfection the art attained previous to the founding of the British Museum and the Jardin des Plantes of Paris. The establishment of the zoölogical collections in these two great institutions must have been its first prominent acknowledgment. The British Museum, the largest institution of its kind in the world, originated in a bequest of Sir HANS SLOANE, who, during his life-time, gathered together objects of natural history and works of art. Collections of the former then formed, and do now, one of the prominent features of the institution. Steadily from the establishment of this Museum in 1753 to the present time the art has increased in importance. Many of the specimens prepared at that time are still in good condition, and will last for an indefinite period. They are especially valuable to the artist of the present day, recording as they do the state of the art at that time, although we must bear in mind that specimens mounted more than a century and a quarter ago, must necessarily show some signs of decay.

The accomplished naturalist, BUFFON, was one of the first naturalists to connect himself with the Jardin des Plantes. His general love of science received a definite impulse towards zoölogy by his appointment, in the year 1739, as Intendent of the Royal Gardens and Museum. Hitherto zoölogy, consisting of a series of unconnected observations and fruitless attempts at classification, had been commonly regarded by the educated reader as a dry study, and by savans as play-work. BUFFON conceived the idea of making it attractive to the first of these classes and securing for it at the same time the respect of the second. Whether or not he was himself a worker in the art of taxidermy, we cannot say, but one thing is certain, namely, that the collections of zoölogy increased rapidly under his administration.

I think it safe to say that there never was an age when nature has not had her students and devotees. True, in the seventeenth century there were but few, so far as we can learn ; but history has not recorded the efforts of the quiet, isolated student. As before stated, we cannot ascertain the exact period when the preservation of animals was first practiced, but we know it originated among ancient tribes. Those who have read CATLIN'S elaborate history of the older Indian tribes, will remember that in his descriptions of Indian ornamentation he mentions the frequency with which portions of wild animals were employed. The heads of foxes, raccoons, woodpeckers and eagles were prepared and stuffed quite naturally, and kept to be worn as decorations on special occasions. The ancient Egyptians employed some of their knowledge in a more progressive manner by embalming the bodies of ibises, cats, crocodiles, common people, and even kings.

All these efforts only illustrate the fondness for preserving, in a natural state, the best of nature's objects. It is safe to say that however good the work may have been at that time, it is far inferior to the style of work to-day. Taxidermy, as an art, has lost nothing, has suffered no decline, has experienced no rapid advancement since its birth as such, and although it has never reached the proud eminence attained by its sister arts, it never stood higher than it stands to-day. When the fact is considered that as an art it has only been practiced less than one hundred and fifty years, it is not strange that it does not stand as high as the other fine arts. The plastic and graphic arts date back many centuries, and have enjoyed the lustre shed upon them by the achievements of a long line of masters. Consider how many art schools have had an existence and how many there are to-day. Even in America there is scarcely a large city which has not one or more. They are composed of skillful masters and devoted students, and receive the support and encouragement of the general public. On the other hand, there has never been a School of Taxidermy; few persons have ever fully enjoyed the privilege of working under a master in the art, and perhaps not more than one-tenth of all the persons who have earnestly desired to learn the art of taxidermy, have been able to succeed in doing so, even in a slight degree. In due time, the Society of American Taxidermists must address itself to the task of imparting information, regularly and systematically.

I know of no art that embraces so many different methods of procedure as taxidermy, but I have never yet known or heard of a method which can claim to be perfection in its practical application. The method for the artist to follow is that one or combination of them which will ensure to a specimen grace and naturalness, combined with durability, and will also produce the desired result in the shortest time and most perfect manner. We may almost say that no two works on taxidermy agree in fundamental principles, yet each author has some peculiar merit, and a true artist should not discard any without thought, simply because their methods may differ from his own. Imagine the sculptor discarding the three pointed calipers because his fellow-workers produced the same results with it ; and yet there are to-day taxidermists who would actually refuse to adopt an improved method if it should chance to be recommended by a rival.

As yet we have had no complete work written on the subject of taxidermy. Of those now in print, each one, almost without exception, has been written by a specialist, who has had but little experience outside of his particular line of work. The most popular work is BROWN'S Manual, it having reached its twenty-first edition in Europe, and has lately been reprinted in America with additional matter. This address will not admit of a discussion of the merits or demerits of any particular work, but for the sake of the rising generation of workers, I feel it my duty to here record the opinion that while some manuals of taxidermy teach gross errors, all are deplorably lacking in thoroughness and systematic detail. A few deserve to be condemned without mercy, and I shall always feel it my duty to assail any work which contains mischievous errors. I think in the future we may reasonably expect at least three elaborate works on this important subject. We will gladly welcome a complete work, written by any thoroughly practical taxidermist, who has had the necessary experience in all branches of the art, and has given satisfactory evidence of his studies.

When I am asked, " Who taught you your art ?" I can only answer, " Nature, and common sense." The average taxidermist is not a close student of nature. Many good artists are closet students only, and their work reveals it plainly to the eye of a true naturalist. The amateur must study living forms if he would succeed. In the past the art has not been taught in a systematized manner, and the obstacles to its advancement have been many, but they are now disappearing. Its progress in the past has, after all, been greater than could be expected, considering the retarding circumstances that have existed.

Only in exceptional cases has taxidermy proven remunerative. The art is not patronized as it should be, but we may reasonably expect that a proper development and improvement will be followed by a new era of prosperity for its followers.

The study of Natural History is becoming very popular, and the interest now manifested in it is in striking contrast with the past. The increase of scientific knowledge has shown the world the importance of gathering together the almost endless forms of life, preserving and storing them where they will safely remain for years to come, and where the student may find them after their living counterparts have ceased to be, or have become inaccessible. We feel greatly encouraged to know that the institutions of America are doing so much in this direction, and that so much more is contemplated. In Europe nearly every large city has a museum of natural history, and in due time we shall be able to say the same of the United States. If we succeed in bringing the art of Taxidermy up to a high state of perfection, such as it has never yet attained, rest assured there will be important work for all our hands to do.

This age is an age of improvement, and we cannot refuse to acknowledge that progression is a working law, visible in all things created. This law is so self-evident that I deem the organization of this Society but the natural result of it. From the day of its formation down to the present time, we have felt great anxiety in its behalf. The occasions have been many when we have asked ourselves, "Will the frail bark that has been launched upon the troubled waters, find strong and steady guiding hands, and survive the storms, or will it sink beneath the waves of opposition?" The possibilities and probabilities have been freely discussed, and the outlook many times has been dark indeed. Yet we have never failed to see some light that has encouraged us to push forward. From the first, our most serious difficulty has been to awaken a lively interest and enthusiasm on the part of taxidermists generally, sufficient to induce them to enter heartily into the plans of the Society. Few men have the courage to embark in a new and doubtful undertaking in which their reputation is at stake. Every artist, whatever may be his line of pursuit, is jealous of his reputation, and in my estimation justly so ; for should it be impaired by any failure or mistake, it is sure to re-act adversely. The painter, the sculptor or the musician regards his reputation as so much capital invested, the loss of which means the loss of position, luxury, and sometimes even comfort.

The art of taxidermy has attracted many zealous and ardent students of nature who follow it for the pleasure it affords them. In point of numbers, amateurs predominate over the professionals, but up to this time it has been the rule with both to jealously guard their knowledge of methods, and to assist no one in learning the art. This course has been considered necessary as a means of self-preservation. Self preservation is the first law of nature, and for this reason it is our duty to be charitable to jealous and exclusive taxidermists, even though we know they are laboring under a mistaken idea. This much I offer in extenuation of the taxidermists who have thought best not to identify themselves with this movement, or have lacked faith in the undertaking. Yet I will not for a moment excuse the men of acknowledged ability who have withheld their support in the hour of need, after they have been fully assured of the meritorious objects and character of this Society. It is more praiseworthy to be a pioneer in any good cause than to be a follower, and every sacrifice we can make in this cause should be a source of pride and pleasure. Years hence when all naturalists, and the admirers of the beautiful forms in animated nature generally, shall accredit this Society with having wrought a great change for the better in the taxidermic art, then I believe that every one whose name stands on the roll to-day will be proud of the fact that he or she was one of the first members, a willing and a working pioneer.

A short account of the formation of this Society may not be out of place, since it is the first of the kind ever formed. Until less than a year ago the taxidermist has been an isolated worker, instinctively excluding himself from his fellow work-men, and, I am sorry to say, too often content in his own little knowledge, and fortified in his own conceit. Such has been the character of the typical taxider-mist, and considering this, is it strange that taxidermy has made but comparatively little advancement?

For a long time I had looked into the past with regrets and into the future with many doubts. I had often compared the present standing of the art with that which I considered possible in the future, and when it was proposed to form a Society, and my judgment was asked, I felt no hesitation in pronouncing it a step in the right direction. We saw at once that much good might follow the establish-ment of a Society of this kind, but there lay in the way so many obstacles, seem-ingly insurmountable, that at first we were fearful that the movement would meet with defeat. But the obstacles merely served to strengthen the determination of the few advocates of the plan. At first the proposition seemed audacious, but as we felt the matter grow in importance decisive steps were taken. On March 14th the few who felt most deeply interested met in an informal meeting, the plan of forming an association was discussed, and it was finally decided to organize a Society at once. At the next meeting officers were elected, a constitution was adopted, a plan of operations agreed upon, and the Society of American Taxider-mists came into existence. Immediate steps were taken to advise American taxidermists of the existence of the Society, and no effort was spared to induce worthy persons to join the organization. Steadily and with rapid strides has the good work gone forward, and the event ushered in by our reception on last evening is the crowning triumph of our labors thus far. Up to this time, the success of the Society has far exceeded the most sanguine expectations of its founders. It has been received with favor by the public, which is a sufficient guarantee of its merits.

As we approach the future, and its possibilities, and pause to think what those who come after will say of their predecessors, we should realize the responsibility resting upon us as a Society. Never before have there been more than three artists associated together, and now that we stand as an associated body, I would charge each member to work earnestly for the success of this organization. I believe that an eventful future lies before us. The Society has made a good beginning, and we should all feel that thus far our efforts have been rewarded. We may well take an honest pride in our undertaking, and do all we can in the future to make each exhibition a grander success than the preceding one. This cannot be done with-out labor, money and tireless perseverance, and whoever may be called upon to discharge the duties of the association, should receive the aid and encourage-ment of every member. I would earnestly impress upon your minds the importance of being patient and hopeful, charitable and self-sacrificing at all times, having the welfare of the Society at heart as well as individual ambition. Above all, beware of jealousy, the green-eyed monster that has caused the defeat of many a noble undertaking.

Though we may not see the immediate results of our enterprise, rest assured that in due time, we shall reap if we faint not. The Society and its exhibitions will earn for taxidermy a position that it has never before held—one of importance and influence. Let us not fear or even hesitate to cast our bread upon the waters, for it will surely return to us. We are entitled to no credit whatever so long as we demand that every dollar spent upon this Society shall come back to us immediately. We must learn to labor and to wait. Instead of allowing half a dozen members to bear the burdens of the Society, every member should consider it a privilege to aid the good work with both time and money. Narrow-mindedness can never accomplish anything great; liberality succeeds in the greatest undertakings.

All of the best naturalists and scientific authorities have no hesitation in expressing the opinion that taxidermy is a fine art, worthy to rank with the best examples of the highest plastic arts. This being a fact, a thorough study of anatomy and muscular development is absolutely necessary if the artist would attain an elevated position in his profession.

Shall we make taxidermy an art that will rank with those which are so eminent? We hold in our hands the answer to this important question. If we do *our* duty, taxidermy will surely accomplish as much in the next ten years as it has during the past century. I believe the spirit of competition will have the desired result. Men of equal ability will strive to excel, and if their efforts are made in a friendly spirit, progression will surely follow. Golden opportunities are within our reach. Let every member be a zealous student of nature in the particular branch he intends following. Let him study living forms with diligence, model the muscular portions whenever possible, and never refuse to profit by the experience of those who have proven by their work that they are entitled to consideration.

In closing, I desire to express, on behalf of the Society, our grateful acknowledgment of the sympathy and support extended in our behalf by the prominent citizens of this city. Our thanks are also due to the press of this city and elsewhere for the kindly interest manifested in the welfare of the Society and for the valuable services they have rendered. We also owe our thanks to the distinguished gentlemen who have so kindly acted as judges of the exhibition and otherwise done so much to make it a success. In tendering them our acknowledgments, I would say that we feel grateful for the guarantee they have given us of their interest in our work. When another year rolls around, may they witness a degree of improvement in our different exhibits which will prove to them and the public that the Society has not labored in vain.